A HEARING GOD HANDBOOK

For A Stiff-Necked People

(I count myself as one)

DAVID LEE TUCKER

A Hearing God Handbook
by David Lee Tucker

ISBN 978-1-63360-358-5

For Worldwide Distribution Printed in USA

Urban Press
PO Box 5044
Williamsburg, VA 23188
+1.757.808.5776
www.urbanpress.us

"Therefore submit to God. Resist the devil and he will flee from you. Draw near to God and He will draw near to you. Cleanse your hands, you sinners; and purify your hearts, you double-minded."
– James 4:7-8

"Now the Lord came and stood and called as at other times, "Samuel! Samuel!" And Samuel answered, "Speak, for Your servant hears."
– 1 Samuel 3:10

"But they did not obey nor incline their ear, but made their neck stiff, that they might not hear nor receive instruction." – Jeremiah 17:23

Contents

Introduction

This handbook documents the process of how God led me to engage Him by hearing His voice—I called, and He answered. It may be called prophecy, or a word of knowledge, or a word of wisdom, but I simply refer to it as hearing God and acting on what you've heard.

When I first began this adventure, I was determined to enter in without textbooks or reference material to guide me—just my Bible and a mindset that said, "I'm here, Lord, and I'm listening." I would then move forward with the certainty that He would respond and guide me to recognize His voice—and then to act on what I heard.

For me, this ultimately became a four-year all-out effort. I admit that at this point in my life, I am not as dedicated, but I am still walking in the results of that period.

Once I started down this path, I learned a great deal from more experienced teachers and have read numerous excellent books on hearing God. Through them, I was amazed and blessed by all the confirmation and additional insight they provided. Hearing God's voice may not be a desire for everybody, but I do believe it is available for all Christ-followers.

This book details the process and some results of my journey, which may or may not be unique for you. I offer it up in response to those who have received a message from me, or whatever it was they felt God had spoken through me to them, and asked, "How do you do that?"

Granted, my experience is not the only way people hear from God. I can be a thick-headed and stiff-necked person, so sometimes it takes a lot for God to break through my defenses. I know of others whose experience in hearing God's voice seems to come much more easily and naturally. Perhaps it is part of a specific gifting. But apparently, they don't have the spiritual earwax buildup I have had.

This process is built on a standard prayer model, but much of it is based on James 4:7-10,

> *"Therefore submit to God. Resist the devil and he will flee from you. Draw near to God and He will draw near to you. Cleanse your hands, you sinners; and purify your hearts, you double-minded. Lament and mourn and weep! Let your laughter be turned to mourning and your joy to gloom. Humble yourselves in the sight of the Lord, and He will lift you up."*

After each chapter I will provide a testimonial of an experience I have had with hearing God.

Important Considerations

If we have the written word of God, why desire to hear God's voice?

Some Christians are certain that with the Bible, there is no further need to hear from God. These are my reasons for our hearing directly from God, consistent with what the Bible teaches.

1. To know that God is with us and is real. Psalm 46:10
2. To be confident that we are in a relationship with God. Song of Solomon 2:8
3. To fully experience a relationship with God. 1 Samuel 3:1-11; 1 Kings 19:11-12; Colossians 1:27
4. To know His voice for guidance and confirmation of His will in our lives. 1 Samuel 16:1-12; Isaiah 30:21; 1 Chronicles 14:14-15; Psalm 32:8-9
5. To truly live the full life God has promised for us. John 10:4-16
6. To more fully experience God's power in our lives. Daniel 10:19

7. To more fully reflect the power of God to a lost world. 1 Corinthians 2:4-5
8. To more fully experience the Body of Christ—act as God's mouthpiece for one another. Matthew 16:17; 1 Samuel 3:9 (Eli helping Samuel); 1 Corinthians 14:26; Acts 2:17; Joel 2:28-32; Numbers 11:29

Two Ears and One Mouth

We've heard the old adage, "We were made with two ears and one mouth for a reason—we should be listening twice as much as we speak." As I read through the Bible, I believe that ratio holds true. God encourages us through His written Word to listen to Him twice as often as He encourages us to speak to Him (someday I may try to prove it). Even when God encourages us to cry out to Him in Scripture, it is often to cry out for God to answer or speak as revealed in Isaiah 58:9 and 11 and Lamentations 3:57

Is that any kind of surprise to us—the possibility that the author and creator of all things should have more to offer to us than we could possibly offer to Him (James 1:5-8)? Yet we still spend the vast majority of our prayer time petitioning and speaking to God. We honor God when we listen to Him and want to hear His voice.

Consider:

- How do we most often demonstrate we care in a relationship? By listening (see 1 Corinthians 13).
- How appreciated do you feel when someone seeks you out for you to listen to them?
- If you had an expert in their field brought in to educate your team, you shouldn't be the ones talking.

As Christians, What is Hearing God for Others?

In 1 Corinthians 14:1, Paul encourages listening and speaking on behalf of God, saying, "*Pursue love, and desire spiritual gifts, but especially that you may prophesy.*" The Greek word here for prophecy is from *prophetes,* meaning *to foretell events, divine, speak under inspiration, or exercise the prophetic office.*

However, I believe New Covenant prophecy is less about specific step-by-step instruction from God or about foretelling the future, but more about engaging with God in a relationship while building up the body of Christ.

Personally, I lean into the aspect of prophesy for the church as speaking under divine inspiration, as Paul continues in 1 Corinthians 14:3, "*But he who prophesies speaks edification and exhortation and comfort to men.*"

What Hearing God Is Not

Let me take a moment to clarify what hearing God is not:

1. It should not be taken as being of equal authority with the Bible, but always consistent with the Bible.
2. It is not about adding anything to Scripture.
3. It is not about justifying an emotional impulse.
4. It should be supported by other Godly wisdom and counsel.
5. It is not about serving your spiritual ego.
6. It is not about performance to impress others with your spirituality.
7. It is not a way to accomplish your agenda.
8. It is not a way to manipulate others.

Next, let me share 10 basic steps that helped me to hear God's voice. Beyond that, if you want more details, insights, testimony, and scriptural support for each step of what I have described, read further.

I hope you experience that which God declared to His servant in 1 Samuel 3:1, *"Then the Lord said to Samuel: 'Behold, I will do something in Israel at which both ears of everyone who hears it will tingle.'"*

Ten Steps to Help You Hear God's Voice

1. Gauge your desire to hear from God.
2. Submit to God by bowing down to God's authority and purpose—dedicating and prioritizing time with Him in a quiet space.
3. Resist the devil by clearing your mind of any anxiousness/concerns/worries/distractions—the other voices. The devil will flee.
4. Draw near to God by making Him your priority—praising and thanking Him for who He is, all that He does, and all that He will do.
5. Cleanse your hands and purify your heart by acknowledging your failures and asking forgiveness. Be totally honest with God. Done! Forgiven! Take it to the bank.
6. Make your requests known. Make your requests about seeking God's wisdom and insights. Remember that this is primarily a time for listening, not speaking. When you conclude asking, *stop talking*!

7. Rhema. Ask God to come and speak to your mind and your spirit. *Be quiet and listen.* Then be a ready writer. Write down what comes into your mind. As any images or words come to mind, ask questions about what they mean and who they may be for. *Make it a dialogue.*
8. Logos. Thank God for speaking and ask Him to speak further through His written word in the Bible. Open your Bible to where you are in your daily reading. Continue reading and see if God, right there, brings further clarity to what you heard. If any words, images, thoughts, or insights jump out. Grab your concordance and conduct a related-word study. Test any *Rhema* against the character of Jesus.
9. Be a doer of the Word. If you sense a message is for you or somebody else, either act on it or share it with those willing to hear. If for others, you don't have to fully understand it. In the original Hebrew, the word obedience means *hearing and doing.* Always pray that God will use His word to speak edification, exhortation, and comfort, which all bring life.
10. Perseverance. Not all of it will land or take root. It takes perseverance to set aside your flesh and hear God more clearly. Wash-rinse-repeat is what is required. The more you faithfully practice this, the more it becomes a practice that God will

reward by His grace according to your faithfulness.

1. Desire

So, the question as a Christ-follower is, "What is my true desire?"

> *"One thing I have desired of the Lord, that will I seek: That I may dwell in the house of the Lord all the days of my life, To behold the beauty of the Lord, and to* ***inquire*** *in His temple"* (Psalm 27:4, emphasis added).

The Greek word for desire means to wish for the longings of one's heart, lust, or appetite. For us, it all starts with *desire*! Yet even before our desire, God desires. James 4:5 says, *"Or do you think that the Scripture says in vain, 'The Spirit who dwells in us yearns jealously?'"*

Both Greek words for *"yearn"* and *"jealousy"* include the concept of desire in their definitions. So, James is expressing a two-fold desire of the Spirit of God.

Essentially, James is saying that God desperately desires His own desire to be the very thing His people desire for other things. He's jealous of whatever the thing we passionately desire. He desires and deserves that same desire for Himself. Why? Because it means our desires have drawn us away from Him. And He desires us to draw near to Him.

The Desire to Know

- *"Whom have I in heaven but You? And there is none upon earth that I **desire** besides You"* (Psalm 73:25).
- *"Delight yourself also in the Lord, And He shall give you the **desires of your heart**"* (Psalm 37:4).
- *"Listen carefully to Me, and eat what is good, And let your **soul delight** itself in abundance. Incline your ear, and come to Me. Hear, and your soul shall live"* (Isaiah 55:2b-3a, emphasis added).

What is it that defines and describes our life in Christ? They are nouns such as faith, hope, belief, and trust. I have found that we most often refer to our Christianity or religion as our *"faith."*

There seems to be a continuum of words that conveys our spiritual state or reality. It is not as linear as I am describing, but the way I see it, it starts with our...

1. desire for God, which then springs into ...
2. hope. We are challenged to step out into ...

3. faith. As we step out, faith grows to ...
4. belief. From there, we extend our ...
5. trust. We then grow in our ...
6. understanding. Maturing into ...
7. confidence. Generating into ...
8. optimism. Which blossoms into staunch ...
9. conviction!

You can't get to a higher spiritual state than staunch conviction, can you? But, actually, there is an even higher state than conviction.

If we are called to testify to the reality of God and our relationship with Christ, we usually talk in terms of our faith—what we believe, how we trust in God, or our conviction in the reality of God.

Yet, the highest standard of a witness is testifying to what we *know*—our *knowledge* of what is true. If we are called to testify in a courtroom, we are called to speak of that which we *know*. If we begin to speak of that which we believe or think, we will hear lawyers scream, "Objection! Irrelevant! Hearsay!"

Definition of knowledge: The fact or condition of knowing something with familiarity gained through experience or association.

I confess that I have fallen into the habit of testifying to others about God's presence in my life by expressing it in terms of faith, belief, or trust. That is likely true of many Christians. Don't get me wrong, for we cannot be in a relationship with God without faith, belief, and trust. In fact, we are saved by faith; it is impossible to please God without it.

Dallas Willard writes, "The difference between belief and knowledge is huge and affects every area of life. Not having knowledge of the central truths of Christianity is certainly one reason for the great disparity between what Christians profess and how they behave."[1]

Still, the truth is that there is so much more that we *know* or can *know* to be true, which is far more powerful when we share, testify, or express our faith. There is a body of knowledge of our God, Jesus, that Scripture encourages us to grow in.

Knowledge in Scripture

- Proverbs 1:7: *"The fear of the Lord is the beginning of knowledge, But fools despise wisdom and instruction."*
- Proverbs 18:15: *"The heart of the prudent acquires knowledge, and the ear of the wise seeks knowledge."*
- Hosea 4:6: *"My people are destroyed for lack of knowledge."*

- 1 Corinthians 1:5: *"That you were enriched in everything by Him in all utterance and all knowledge."*
- Ephesians 3:19: *"to know the love of Christ which passes knowledge; that you may be filled with all the fullness of God."*
- Ephesians 4:13: *"Till we all come to the unity of the faith and of the knowledge of the Son of God, to a perfect man."*
- Colossians 1:9: *"That you may be filled with the knowledge of His will in all wisdom and spiritual understanding."*

Where it all begins is with a desire in our hearts to grow in knowing God in an intimate, dynamic, active, and interactive relationship; to know Him beyond head knowledge; to commune with and to abide in a relationship with Jesus.

Mark Daniel in *Prayer Altars* writes, "How do we get revelation of the One True God? By communing with Him. It is in that communion that we begin to see Him for who He is. We begin to know His heart and His character. We come to know Him, put our hope in Him, and give Him our hearts and our love."[2]

How did Jesus know to do and say

the things He did? He communed with the Father. He could hear and see the Father. As I detailed in my book, *Emptied,* Jesus is our model. That is what I see in Scripture and what I signed up for as a Christ-follower.

For many Christians, the written word of God is enough. They don't believe there is any need for more than that. I don't doubt that it is actually enough. If your deep God-centered desires lie elsewhere, exploring how to hear God's voice may not be for you.

For me, this is not rocket science—fairly simple but certainly not easy. A genuine desire means you are willing to prioritize dedicated time and effort, and to step out in courageous faith to explore a deeper, more active, and even more interactive relationship with God.

Francis Chan writes what's necessary for a deeper prayer experience in his book, *Beloved.* "If you want to have a robust, intimate prayer life, you are going to have to sacrifice for it, and you are going to have to work at it. But there is no pursuit more worthy or rewarding."[3]

What follows is a brief description of my beginnings.

How Real Is My God?

The question was a scary one. How *real* do I *really* think my God *really* is?

At one point, I had been following Jesus Christ for about 20 years. All along, I was growing in the knowledge of Jesus and experiencing Him in real ways. I loved that when I called upon the Lord, He'd respond as David described in Psalm 116:1-2, *"I love the Lord, because He has heard My voice and my supplications. Because He has inclined His ear to me, Therefore I will call upon Him as long as I live."*

But, at that point, I seemed to hit a wall. There was something more I was looking for. *How big was my God? What kind of testimony to the reality of God in my life did I really have? If someone asked me how I could be certain God was real, what could I say?*

Where in my life was the reality of verses like Jeremiah 33:3, *"Call to me and I will answer you, and will tell you great and hidden things that you have not known"?*

Or Psalm 85:8, *"Let me hear what God the LORD will speak, for he will speak peace to his people, to his saints; but let them not turn back to folly."?*

Or John 8:47, "*Whoever is of God hears the words of God. The reason why you do not hear them is that you are not of God."?*

Or John 10:27, "*My sheep hear my voice, and I know them, and they follow me."?*

Before heading off on a short-term mission trip, I made a decision. I was going to use the time to begin treating God as more real than ever before. How would I do that? I planned to begin reading through the Bible again. (Pretty clever, huh?)

I had previously worked my way through the Bible several times, but this time I was going to pray beforehand, with a determination to engage God and *listen for His voice*—and then listen further by reading His written word.

If I could clear the clutter from my mind and truly believe God was real, whatever came into my head would be His voice. I determined that if my God is big and real enough, He would speak. I would write it down and then act on what God said. Little did I know what I was getting into.

One of the biggest concerns was how I would know that what was coming into my head was from God? I decided what I was hearing had to pass three tests if I was to be confident that it was from God:

- Was the voice I was hearing in

my head consistent with God's written Word, the Bible?

- Was the voice I was hearing for myself or for others consistent with 1 Corinthians 14:3—speaking edification, exhortation, and comfort to others?
- Was it consistent with the character of Christ, utilizing the fruit of the Spirit found in Galatians 5:22-23: love, joy, peace, longsuffering, kindness, goodness, faithfulness, gentleness, self-control?

As I committed significant time and energy to this, God responded, and I saw the reality of James 4:8, *"Draw near to God and He will draw near to you"* and Hebrews 11:6, *"[God] is a rewarder of those who diligently seek Him."* God was speaking, and as much as I was faithful in being a "doer" of His word, God began to deliver more than I could handle. God seemed to be saying, "You want it, you got it!"

Isaiah 44:3 says, *"I will pour water upon him who is thirsty."* The Hebrew phrase for 'pour water' is *yatsaq mayim*. It indicates a pouring over of refreshing waters, but with an almost violent undertone. At times, I felt like I was drinking from the proverbial firehose. He was bringing issues, people, and situations to mind, speaking into my own life and others' lives. Would I be receptive and His faithful emissary?

It was a tremendous time of stretching my faith not only to act on what God was speaking into my own life, but also to speak into others' lives. Let me say that on the extrovert-to-introvert personality spectrum, I fall on the introvert side. I basically find human interaction exhausting. For me, this was a challenge.

Offering what I believed were God's words of life, peace, joy, and comfort to others was challenging enough. This was often well received. But, more than a few times, people gave me a confused look, not knowing what I was talking about. That was easy enough to understand—I had heard wrong, so what I shared didn't mean anything to them. I encouraged them to put what I had said on the shelf or throw it out altogether. On numerous occasions, people came back later, excited that the words had become something meaningful to them.

A real challenge, however, was the confrontation of difficult issues—bad behavior, sin, addictions, confusion, unfaithfulness, unkindness, coarse language, etc. God seemed to be calling me to confront these things in others (God wasn't shy about bringing up my own issues either).

The truth is that Jesus was able to do it. Jesus confronted without condemning, staying true to His character. I realized that I had to know what Jesus would say and how He would say it. They were not my words and voice but His words and voice. This required knowing Christ's true character and abiding in who He is.

The point of sharing this experience is that if God wanted me to address a difficult situation, He wanted to tell me how to do it in a way consistent with the character of Christ. For those occasions when I have truly sought out His words and voice, I have seen God touch lives in amazing ways. However, even when I am completely confident I have acted as Jesus's voice to others, it does not always have the impact I hoped for.

Jesus was not always able to have the impact He desired. Even with words that were good, righteous, and true, people turned away from Jesus (e.g., the rich young ruler) because the message was too difficult. Still, I am convinced that if I am willing to put in the time and effort, any message can be effectively conveyed with the rich, full-nectar medley of all the fruit of the Spirit—the full character of Jesus.

The truth, however, is that this does not come easily, at least not in my experience. When the disciples failed to heal the boy as recorded in Matthew 17:14-21, they asked Jesus why they had failed. He replied, "*Because of your unbelief . . . However, this kind does not go out except by prayer and fasting*" (verses 20-21). I believe part of this answer for us is not operating in the natural but earnestly engaging God for the words and ways He directs us to respond, which is always consistent with the character of Christ.

Dallas Willard writes, "However firm we may be in our convictions, we do not become overbearing, contemptuous, hostile, or defensive. We know that Jesus himself would not do so, because we cannot help people in that way. He had no need of it, nor do we."[4]

How does this all happen, and is this kind of God interaction for today? I say yes and agree with Jamie Winship when he writes in his book, *Living Fearless*, "This abiding, life-union with Jesus is available to us today and includes all the fullness of the Godhead; spiritual fruitfulness; the fullness of the words, love, and joy of the Father; answered prayer; and the glory and honor of God."[5]

Testimonials of Hearing God's Voice

Let me provide a sampling of my experiences with hearing God and acting upon what I've heard.

Each experience is an example of God using a member of His Body to speak on His behalf, letting us know that He is there and desires to be active in our lives in a very real and interactive way.

These are just some episodes of when I listened to God and faithfully spoke what I had heard or seen. There are many more. But

I have not always been faithful, and on many occasions, what I believed I was hearing but did share obviously hadn't landed with the impact I would have hoped for. Many times, the real impact is not immediate. I trust that, if it is done out of genuine love for others and in service to the King, God will not allow it to come back void.

For me, it has taken a long time to listen, and then test and act on what I'm hearing. This is likely because God has graciously allowed me to go at the pace I'm willing to go.

Much of what I've learned has been shaped by the quiet, dedicated time I've spent with God in the study of Scripture to grow in the knowledge of His character, and intently listening to recognize and trust His voice. Eventually, I've come to the point where I do hear God a little more "on the fly." Here is the first of a few examples of my experience.

Testimonial 1
Blessed Assurance

It was an early Sunday morning at the "old" church building. A small group of men gathered together once more to pray. Our hearts were united—set on pursuing and seeking a deeper, more relational, and powerful prayer experience.

Our group met in the church's makeshift "prayer room"—one third of a meeting room known as "The Lounge" that could be split into three smaller meeting areas. We quietly settled in as the worship prelude from our early traditional service drifted in, adding to the peaceful atmosphere. There was no rush to engage as we set our minds on God and let the cares we carried in slip away.

We let the choir-led worship of the classic hymn "Blessed Assurance" waft over us as we invited the Holy Spirit to join us. We then began to share what God was putting on our hearts and minds concerning the desires we shared for His kingdom, God's designs for our vision for a new church building—awakenings, revival, and dare we say, "miracles"?

Then our spiritual sage, Dr. Wayne Detzler, shared a deep desire he had held for 50 years in ministry. His voice quivered with emotion as he stated, "One day, I long to see someone actually raised from the dead!"

Whoa! I literally rolled my closed eyes. *That is way beyond my faith!* But we continued praying for a few more minutes before our peaceful prayers were shattered.

Boom! A door into the lounge burst open, and loud, anxious voices were suddenly calling out directions. We opened our eyes and snapped our heads around to see a group of men at the other end of the lounge struggling to carry something heavy into the room. We stood up and exchanged stunned looks. *What is going on?*

The men cleared an area in the center of the lounge and there they laid down another man on the floor. His face was ashen and still. Amongst the anxious commotion, there was no movement. We looked at one another, and someone whispered, "It's Carl Benson."

Others rushed in: a nurse and a doctor from the congregation. They began feverishly performing CPR to revive Carl.

Our prayer group stood there stunned. *We should be doing something!* I thought. Like a slap to the face, someone called out, "Come on. Let's pray!" We all fell to our knees and began feverishly intervening for Carl's life.

A portable defibrillator was brought

into the room. The doctor began to shock Carl's heart to revive him. With my eyes closed, I heard a buzzing, then a beeping, then the call, "Clear"–and then that sound 'Pumf'. Carl didn't respond. They repeated the process again: buzzing, beeping, "Clear," Pumf. Nothing. They repeated it several more times with a growing level of concern—even panic. Things were not going well.

The urgency of our prayers increased as some of us began praying more vocally. While this struggle continued, I prayed, *Please God, come and intervene. Come and keep Carl alive.*

Then, as the medical team's anxious words sounded more like surrender, I thought, *He's gone!* I cringed with resignation. *It's over.* The realization that Carl was dead was sinking in. The dark sadness began to take hold.

> *"That I may know Him and the power of His resurrection, and the fellowship of His sufferings, being conformed to His death, if, by any means, I may attain to the resurrection from the dead"* Philippians 3:10-11).

But our group fought against the hopelessness and pressed on in our faith, praying for God to rescue Carl, resisting the idea that Carl was gone. Our prayers changed to, "God, resurrect Carl" and similar supplications, begging God to do *this*.

Suddenly, the title of the worship song the congregation had just sung flashed into my mind as God spoke to my spirit. His "Blessed Assurance" swept over me. I rejoiced with soaring confidence. *God will do this!* For me, this was a never-before-experienced feeling of certainty that God would actually do something momentous in that very moment as we prayed.

Then came a loud cough, followed by more coughing and deep gasping for air. Sounds of surprise, great relief, and calls of thanks to God filled the room from those who had been working on Carl. I could hear the comments from the medical team saying that they were certain Carl was gone and had given up on reviving him when God's spark of life caused Carl to convulse back into this realm.

Carl was dead, but God had raised him from the dead. He was alive! (It turned out that the doctor was a professor of emergency medicine at Yale. He later shared that he was "astounded" that Carl was alive.)

This testimony is about God's miraculous power to raise a man from the dead. Praise God! At the same time, God chose to answer Dr. Detzler's desire to see God's resurrection power realized. All who were gathered there had the privilege of being part of this miracle. And for me, it was the first time I experienced this kind of God's *rhema*: His word spoken directly to my mind/spirit in glowing neon letters, causing my faith and assurance in His power to soar to new heights.

The hymn "Blessed Assurance" concerns our assurance of salvation. Yet, what are we saved from? Sin and death. The second verse declares God's revelation with, *"Perfect submission, perfect delight, Visions of rapture now burst on my sight; Angels descending, bring from above Echoes of mercy, whispers of love."* And so, we sing the soaring refrain, *"This is my story, this is my song, praising my Savior all the day long!"*

~~~

So, what's next? Where do we go from here to start hearing God's voice if we have the desire to do so?
~~~

2. Submit to God

James 4:7a – *"Therefore submit to God."*

The Greek word for *submit* is to *subordinate; reflexively, to obey*. It is from *hupo-tasso*, a Greek military term meaning *to arrange troops in a military fashion under the command of a leader.*

What does it mean to submit to God? God does not twist our arm. It means that I am willing to subordinate my agenda and priorities to Him. I will bend my will to God's will. Jesus declared in Luke 22:42, *"Nevertheless not My will, but Yours, be done."*

In this book, submitting to God means dedicating and prioritizing time with Him in a quiet space. I must be willing to give up other priorities—food, sleep, passions, and other pleasures in order to engage with my God.

Why does it start with submission? It's because it immediately checks your heart's motivation to hear from God. Is it so you can impress others with your heightened spirituality? Does it serve your spiritual ego? Do you view it as a way to manipulate others? Is it a way to accomplish your agenda?

Submitting to God immediately checks all that self-serving baggage at the door. It also indicates that you are willing to be attentive and obedient to whatever God has to say. Being obstinate and unwilling to submit to God was often referred to in the Old Testament as being stiff-necked.

Loosen Up!

It's a gentle nudge, a passing thought, a whisper in my ear: "Speak to that person, send a message, make a call, do something for Me. Be My messenger."

God's voice is described in 1 Kings as "a still small voice." When someone whispers, we often have to twist our necks and lean toward them to hear. We want to hear what they are saying, so we make an effort to draw as close as we can so we don't miss a word. People skilled in public speaking use this method to quiet their voice before making a point, drawing the audience closer to truly listening when the major point is delivered.

We find Jeremiah declaring in Jeremiah 17:23, *"But they did not obey nor incline their ear, but made their neck stiff, that they might not hear nor receive instruction."* Later in Jeremiah 19:14-15, *"Jeremiah said to all the people, 'Thus says the Lord of hosts, the God of Israel: 'Behold, I will bring on this city and on all her towns all the doom that I have pronounced against it, because they have stiffened their necks that they might not hear My words.'"*

The original Hebrew, translated as "stiff neck" seems to indicate that Jeremiah is talking about "stiff-necked persons acting like they have a stiff neck" or "obstinate people acting particularly difficult." What were the people doing? They were not inclining their ear to hear the Lord's instruction. They were unwilling to twist their neck and lean in to hear God's voice. How often do I do that? How often do you do it? I can be a difficult person, wanting to do what I want to do. I suppose we are all like that. The Holy Spirit is speaking, but I won't lean over to come close to hear His whisper.

In Hebrews 3:7-9, the writer warns, *"Therefore, as the Holy Spirit says* (speaks): *'Today, if you will hear* [comprehend by hearing] His voice (from the Greek *phōnē* where we get the English word *phone), do not harden your hearts as in the rebellion, in the day of trial in the wilderness, where your fathers tested Me, tried Me, and saw My works forty years."* God's spoken word has been proven, and He continues to speak. Incline your heart—and loosen your neck—to hear His voice.

Matthew 5:19 records, *"Then Jesus answered and said to them, 'Most assuredly, I say to you, the Son can do nothing of Himself, but what He sees the Father do; for whatever He does, the Son also does in like manner.'"*

And then later in verse 30, Jesus said, *"I can of Myself do nothing. As I hear, I judge; and My judgment is righteous, because I do not seek My own will but the will of the Father who sent Me."*

Jesus repeatedly encouraged *"those who have ears to hear, listen!"* Jesus always deferred His will to the Father's will. In that way, He could more clearly hear and see the things the Father desired to show and say to Him. Beyond just surface hearing in Luke 9:44, Jesus implored His disciples to, *"Let these words sink down into your ears. . ."*

So, I will pray, "Thank You, Father, for loving me even as I willfully ignore Your voice and go about seeking my own will. But, on this day, I will soften my heart and limber up my neck to twist, turn, and lean in to hear Your voice guiding me and directing me to follow Your will. And may I discover what Job describes in Job 26:14, *"Indeed these are the mere edges of His ways, And how small a whisper we hear of Him! But the thunder of His power who can understand?"*

So, loosen up!

~~~

Pop Goes the Miracle

I've had interesting experiences over the years while praying for people in different circumstances, and on several occasions, the word "Pop" has come into my mind.
~~~

Testimonial 2
Pop Goes the Balloon

My friend Mark was diagnosed with a cancerous brain tumor and was going in for surgery. Just before the surgery, our church men's group gathered around him for prayer.

We obviously prayed for his healing, and as we prayed, an image of a balloon came into my mind. Then I saw the word "Pop." But the balloon did not burst. It had a small hole in it and was slowly withering to something like a shriveled fig. I was led to Isaiah 34:4, where the prophet was declaring judgment against God's enemies: *"All the stars in the sky will be dissolved and the heavens rolled up like a scroll; all the starry host will fall like withered leaves from the vine, like shriveled figs from the fig tree."*

This was the first time that God's *rhema* as an image came into my mind as I was praying—an image that seemed connected to our prayers. Yet, the image didn't quite match how we were all praying—that God would just make the tumor disappear.

When we concluded, I shared this

with Mark. He squinted and shrugged, "Well, okay." (He later shared that he did not take it as positive, thinking it meant something about the air going out of his life. He was not encouraged by what I shared.)

Mark went into surgery. When the surgeon opened him up, they were certain to find a solid mass that would be a challenge to cleanly remove from the brain tissue. Their hope was to scrape it all out, leaving only good tissue. The most reassuring comment to his family at the end of the surgery would probably have been, "We *believe* we got it all."

But when the surgeon went in, they were shocked to find a cavity with a wrinkled blob of tissue inside. The best way they could describe the tumor was as a 'deflated balloon.' It was as though it had been filled with fluid, then popped and drained, leaving a shriveled mass disconnected from any other tissue. This allowed it to be easily removed. After testing the surrounding area, they declared Mark clean and free of cancer. Awesome!

Note: Years later, the cancer did return, and the Lord brought Mark home. But Mark enjoyed many additional years with friends and family, being a powerful witness to God's loving faithfulness.

~~~

So, what's next? Where do we go from here to start hearing God's voice once we have submitted to God?
~~~

3. Resist the Devil

James 4:7b – "*Resist the devil and he will flee from you.*"

The Greek word for *resist* is *antistēte: to set against, to withstand, to oppose, to stand against.*

My Bodyguard

In the 1980 movie *My Bodyguard*, a weakling kid is being bullied by kids bigger than he is. The weakling agrees to help a bigger/older kid rebuild his motorcycle. In exchange, the older boy agrees to be his bodyguard.

So, the next time the bullies harass the boy, they are surprised when he stands up and resists, and the bullies run off in fear. Why? The bullies see the weakling resisting because he has someone even more powerful and threatening than they are standing behind him.

This is why submitting to God and resisting the devil are so connected. Once we submit to God, we rely on His power and authority, and that is what the devil sees in us when we resist. The coward then flees in terror.

It is why the demons always trembled when Jesus confronted them. They had to bend to God's will and authority. James 2:19 confirms, *"You believe that there is one God. You do well. Even the demons believe—and tremble!"*

When engaging God to hear His voice, what will the enemy do to defeat us? He will amplify other voices that plant seeds of doubt and unworthiness, clogging our spiritual ears with worldly messages and concerns. In order to hear God's voice, resisting the devil means clearing your mind of anxiety, worries, doubts, or other distractions—those are the other voices vying for God's attention.

Jamie Winship in *Living Fearless* writes, "When you speak truth, Satan moves away from you because you are submitting to God and therefore resisting the enemy."[6]

It's your choice, with the Spirit's power, to replace the lies with the truth. In the light of truth, the bully is disarmed and disoriented and will flee. Remind yourself of your value with these verses:

- 1 John 4:19: *"We love Him because He first loved us."*
- 2 Corinthians 5:21: *"For He made Him who knew no sin to be sin for us, that we might become the righteousness of God in Him."*

- Romans 8:38-39: "*For I am convinced that neither death nor life, neither angels nor demons, neither the present nor the future, nor any powers, neither height nor depth, nor anything else in all creation, will be able to separate us from the love of God that is in Christ Jesus our Lord.*"
- Ephesians 2:10: "*For we are His workmanship, created in Christ Jesus for good works, which God prepared beforehand that we should walk in them.*"

Testimonial 3
Pop Goes the Ear

Before a weekly youth meeting at church, one of the leaders came into our prayer meeting. The leader is an accomplished musician who teaches music and was scheduled to lead worship at the upcoming youth retreat. He was also scheduled to give the message to the teenagers that evening.

Unfortunately, the leader had been suffering for weeks with some kind of ear problem, causing significant pain and loss of hearing in one ear. The doctors couldn't find a remedy for the situation. Obviously, for someone who plays and directs music, this was a major problem and a real source of frustration.

The prayer team came around him. He was 'all in' for having God show up in whatever way He chose during our prayer time. He shared that the doctors were at a loss and hoped that what was happening in his ear would open on its own. If not, then he would be facing surgery.

As we were praying, the word "pop"

came into my mind once again. I was led to Psalm 40:6, *"Sacrifice and offering You did not desire; my ears You have opened. Burnt offering and sin offering You did not require."*

We prayed, focusing on that verse, and concluded our prayer by laying hands on him and praying for God's healing to be complete—that God would indeed break through and the damage that was blocking his ear would completely "pop" open.

He was encouraged but experienced no further relief. His ear was still blocked. He then went right from our prayer time to sharing a message at the youth meeting. As I drove home, I somehow felt certain we'd be hearing from the leader about that "pop."

Later that evening, I received a text from a prayer team leader who had heard the youth leader speak. When the leader had concluded his message, he told the kids what the prayer team had prayed over him earlier. He then testified that with about five minutes left in the message, his ear "popped" open and his hearing was fully restored. His report after being part of a powerful youth retreat was that his hearing was 100%.

~~~

So, what's next? Where do we go from here to start hearing God's voice once we have resisted the Devil?
~~~

4. Draw Near to God

James 4:8a – *"Draw near to God and He will draw near to you."*

You draw near to God by making Him your priority, praising and thanking Him for who He is, all that He does, and all that He will do.

Generally, what is the purpose of drawing near to someone or something? When we draw near, we aim to come closer and become more intimate, so we can engage with them more effectively.

Imagine two boxers in a ring, and neither will draw near enough to land a punch. There would be two men punching and jabbing the air, accomplishing nothing.

Picture being alongside a busy freeway, trying to have a meaningful conversation with someone on the other side. Trucks and cars are whizzing by, and that person is only catching a few words of what you say. You need to cross the highway to communicate more effectively.

I participated in a short-term medical mission to an isolated area of Panama. We set up in an abandoned building, and villagers came from miles, mostly walking, to get the medical care they needed. Some showed up at the end of the day after walking all day. They had to do what it took to draw near to access the clinic's healing treatments. Jesus always allowed those who wanted to be healed to draw near to Him.

Remember also that drawing near is vital if you are going to engage, but it is not actual engagement. When an army draws near the enemy, 'drawing near' does not mean engaging the enemy in battle; it means coming close enough to fight the enemy effectively. When we draw near, it is about the effort to come close enough to fully engage another.

John Mulinde in *Prayer Altars* wrote of King David, "God drew near to David as David's heart drew near to God, and David forever remained the standard by which God measured the kings of Jerusalem and Israel."[7]

So, James 4:8 says, *"Draw near to God and He will draw near to you."* I am not into spiritual formulas because just when I think I've figured out how God works, He does something new. Jesus Himself acted in ways unique to each situation. However, I am going to propose something that is akin to a formula:

A legitimate spiritual dynamic seen throughout Scripture: If we humbly and boldly draw near to God, He responds by drawing near to us.

Spiritual Two-Step

Drawing near to God is like a dance. This simile has been demonstrated time and again in my Christian experience. From the moment I first heard the Gospel, God has made Himself known. He has made His love for me and for you known. His desire for us is made evident.

Romans 1:20 says, *"For the invisible things of him from the creation of the world are clearly seen, being understood by the things that are made, his eternal power and Godhead; so that they are without excuse."*

He stands with open arms (being the eternal gentleman), waiting for us to take the step towards him, and then He responds. He does not impose himself.

The Greek word for prayer (*pros-yoo-khom-ahee*) has the root words of *pros*, which is a preposition of direction (forward, toward, alongside of, or drawing close to) and *yoo-khom-ahee*, which is then about making your wishes known.

Prefer Speaking Face to Face

The Apostle John stated his preference for speaking face to face in 3 John 13-14, *"I had many things to write, but I do not wish to write to you with pen and ink; but I hope to see you shortly, and we shall speak face to face."*

While meeting this way with God, the psalmist recorded in Psalm 27:8, *"When You said, 'Seek My face,' my heart said to You, 'Your face, Lord, I will seek.'"*

Paul also wrote in 1 Corinthians 13:12, *"For now we see in a mirror, dimly, but then face to face. Now I know in part, but then I shall know just as I also am known."*

What's Required?

So, what's required of us to draw near to God? The answer lies in the Scriptures surrounding verse 8 in James chapter 4, particularly the concept of drawing near to God. James 4:8b-10 states, *"Cleanse your hands, you sinners; and purify your hearts, you double-minded. Lament and mourn and weep! Let your laughter be turned to mourning and your joy to gloom. Humble yourselves in the sight of the Lord, and He will lift you up."*

Earlier, James encouraged his readers to draw near to God. In verse 7, he wrote, "Therefore." What's the "there" for? It's there because the previous verses talk of the entanglements of the world, and James was describing how to escape all that. It's about pushing aside the stuff that stands between God and us.

Mark Daniel in *Prayer Altars* writes this regarding drawing near to God,

> The Scriptures teach us in James 4:8, "Draw near to God, and he will draw near to you." How do we come near to God? Psalm 100:4 says, "Enter his gates with thanksgiving,

> and his courts with praise!" We draw near to God with thanksgiving and praise. The Scriptures also say that God inhabits the praises of His people (Psalm 22:3, KJV). "Inhabits" implies that God comes and dwells with; He moves toward the praises of His people. We can trust that as we draw near to God, He will draw near to us.[8]

Even as we enter in with praise and thanksgiving to invite Him in, the praise and thanksgiving also work to cleanse and humble ourselves.

Testimonial 4
Pop Goes the Back

One of our pastors had come to a prayer meeting with terrible back pain. He was a young guy, but looked like an old man, bent over and hobbling.

We prayed for him, and I saw the word "pop" come into my mind. So, we prayed that God would "pop" his back into place and heal him completely. I was led to Acts 14:9-10, "This man heard Paul speaking. Paul, observing him intently and seeing that he had faith to be healed, said with a loud voice, "Stand up straight on your feet!" And he leaped and walked." We prayed that it would happen for him.

Unfortunately, our pastor didn't immediately straighten up and leap. We left the meeting with him still bent over and in pain.

However, when I got home, I got a message from the pastor, excitedly sharing that after the meeting, just as he was about to climb into his car, his back distinctly 'popped'. His back was healed, and the pain was completely gone. Pop!

~~~

What's next? Where do we go from here to hearing God's voice? What's required of us to draw close enough to God to hear His voice?
~~~

5. Cleanse Your Hands; Purify Your Heart

James 4:8b-10 – *"Cleanse your hands, you sinners; and purify your hearts, you double-minded. Lament and mourn and weep! Let your laughter be turned to mourning and your joy to gloom. Humble yourselves in the sight of the Lord, and He will lift you up."*

Let's look more closely at what it means to draw near in relationship to God. What does God say is required? What's the recipe? I believe it is found in James 4:8b-10 that we saw in the last chapter.

Cleanse your hands, you sinners.

What does that mean? The Greek word for *hands* actually refers to the actions we perform with our hands. We need to, as they say, "clean up our act." But wait? I thought our sins were forgiven? They are, but this passage does not refer to our salvation; it speaks instead of drawing near to God in a relationship. It's about dealing with those things we make a greater priority than our relationship with God. It's like being told to wash your hands of the dirty things you do before you come to the table.

Purify your hearts, you double-minded.

The Greek word for *heart* refers to that which is central to us. When we purify water, we're removing the harmful substances that don't belong there. Likewise, we are to be single-minded and pure about what is important to us. It's about clearing out that which blocks our ability to hear Him. Be completely honest with God. Jamie Winship says, "That means if we're not willing to speak in truth, he's not talking. Or rather, he is talking, but we can't hear him. Those are the ground rules."[9]

I am fully convinced of God's goodness and that the fruit of the Spirit displays the beautiful character of God. I am convinced that Jesus' declaration in Matthew 10:10 is true: He came so that we would have an abundant life. However, verse 9 has been a troublesome verse for me. It seems that James has presented something both comforting and confusing.

> *"Lament and mourn and weep! Let your laughter be turned to mourning and your joy to gloom."*

This is how we draw close to God, by being sad and pathetic? Taking a closer look, I believe this refers to the things James says we need to cleanse and purify, by letting go of those things that draw us away from God. They, however, are things that have grown important to us, increasingly relying on them to get us through life. Letting go of those things will likely be hard and even painful.

As an extreme example, let's consider a heroin addiction. Verse 9 is an amazing description of what someone goes through during withdrawal as they break this habit.

Lament and mourn and weep!

It's like a smorgasbord of anguish! In the Greek lament means to endure labors and hardships—to feel afflicted and miserable. To mourn means to experience great loss. To weep is a sign of pain and grief. All this represents something that has become physically, emotionally, and spiritually of high importance to someone, only to be ripped away.

Philippians 3:8, "*Yet indeed I also count all things loss for the excellence of the knowledge of Christ Jesus my Lord, for whom I have suffered the loss of all things, and count them as rubbish, that I may gain Christ.*" To suffer loss in the Greek means to sustain damage, or to receive injury.

John Mark Comer in *Practicing the Way* says this about dying to self, "We will have to die a thousand deaths, but it will absolutely be worth it. With Jesus, you always gain far more than you give up."[10]

Let your laughter be turned to
mourning and your joy to gloom.

What once brought you euphoria, laughter, and joy is now a source of mourning and gloom. Addiction to sin leads to a painful hangover when you are left face-to-face with an even more dismal reality that this kind of medication is a short-lived relief, ultimately inflicting greater pain. Finally, James echoes Jesus's words in verse 10, saying,

"Humble yourselves in the sight of the Lord, and He will lift you up."

Come to your knees as you draw near, and God will lift you up. If we humble ourselves, what will God do? Draw near to lift us up. But the Greek for "lift up" is not just to pick up but to lift on high. It is to exalt, to raise to the very summit of opulence and prosperity, to raise up to dignity, honor and happiness. Matthew 23:12, *"And whosoever shall exalt himself shall be abased; and he that shall humble himself shall be exalted."*

James says that a process of cleansing: purifying, lamenting, mourning, weeping, and humbling needs to occur. But what exactly can we do to draw near so God will respond? How do we draw near? What does that look like to draw near to God? What exactly can we do? What did it look like in the gospels? The people then had the advantage of Jesus Christ's physical presence, whom they could seek out and draw near to.

Envision the many scenes in the gospels where individuals like the centurion, the blind men who followed Jesus into the house, the Samaritan woman, Zacchaeus climbing the tree, the paralytic who was passed down through the roof, the rich young ruler who came running and knelt before Jesus, and all the crowds that followed Jesus, came from great distances, through towns and cities, up hills and mountains and to the shores and out into the sea. In almost every case of healing, people made an effort to draw near to Jesus.

Unfortunately, we do not have a physical being to which we can draw near that demonstrates our desire and determination to move towards. Therefore, if you ask most people what it means to *draw near* to God, they would probably say: pray and read your Bible.

Those activities, while vital for engaging with God, are not necessarily part of drawing near to God. If we feel that our prayer life and Bible study are not fruitful and we still feel distant from God, it may be because we are trying to engage without first drawing near to God.

I believe that the tangible effort to draw near to God today can be found through exercising certain other spiritual disciplines. In Dallas Willard's book *The Spirit of The Disciplines*, he divides 15 disciplines into two groups: the seven spiritual disciplines of *abstinence* and the eight spiritual disciplines of *engagement*.[11]

- Disciplines of Abstinence – Solitude, Silence, Fasting, Frugality, Chastity, Secrecy, Sacrifice

- Disciplines of Engagement – Prayer, Study, Worship, Celebration, Service, Fellowship, Confession, Submission

My premise is that all spiritual disciplines are about engaging with God. You are either about eliminating "stuff" that blocks your relationship with God (example: solitude) or you are initiating things to enter into communication/relationship with God (example: prayer).

What Willard calls the disciplines of abstinence, I'd say are all about *drawing near* so that you can then more fully and intimately *engage with God.* Each discipline is an effort to remove the things of this world that bombard our senses, demanding our attention and exhausting our physical, emotional, and spiritual energy, leaving little for God.

Francis Chan puts it this way, "Cultivating a hunger for God's presence and power in your life might mean starving yourself of lesser things."[12]

I'd prefer to call the disciplines of abstinence, the *disciplines of drawing near.* Each is an effort to abstain from the desires of this world to shift to the desire to engage with God. Once again, they include: solitude, silence, fasting, frugality, chastity, secrecy, and sacrifice.

Each of these requires a more detailed

explanation, so I would highly recommend Willard's excellent book. For now, suffice it to say that God recognizes our desire to draw near to Him when we make engaging with Him the priority over our other desires and interests.

~~~

Knives Out

When praying and listening for God to speak, as mentioned earlier, I keep in mind that whatever I believe I have heard should align with the fruit of the Spirit and should align with 1 Corinthians 14:3—it should be edifying, exhorting, and comforting. So, what do you do with images that seem disturbing?
~~~

Testimonial 5
Playing with a Knife

I was praying in advance of a youth group meeting, after which the prayer team would offer to pray for individuals. While I was praying, I got a distinct image of someone lying down and taking a knife to repeatedly stab at their abdomen. The person was not actually stabbing, but looked as if they were practicing.

I dismissed it. *How could I share this with a teenager? How could this possibly fit with the fruit of the Spirit and with 1 Corinthians 14:3?*

That evening at the end of the service, we invited the teens to come forward for prayer and I was encouraged to see so many teens respond. As one young man approached me, I immediately had the image of the "knife stabbing" come back to my mind. I thought, *Oh no. How can I say this? Should I say this?* I got a clear confirmation to proceed.

When I asked him what I could pray for, he mentioned that there was difficulty at home. The parents had split up, and there was a lot of dysfunction. So I prayed for God's healing and restoration, and then I shared what God laid on me for someone, believing it might be for him.

I told him of the stabbing imagery and was led to add Psalm 22:19-21, *"But You, O Lord, do not be far from Me; O My Strength, hasten to help Me! Deliver me from the sword, my precious life from the power of the dog. Save Me from the lion's mouth and from the horns of the wild oxen!"* I shared my conviction that, though he was under attack, God's hand was intervening to prevent him from being "stabbed." (I assumed that the attack was something spiritual and psychological in nature.)

He looked at me in shock and became emotional, admitting that for some time in his room as he lay in bed, he had been "playing" with a knife and fantasizing about stabbing himself. At that point, he knew that God was watching and making it clear that this was not His plan for him. He broke down and was reassured by the reality of God's love amid the family dysfunction.

I urged him to share this with his Christian mom, and they were both greatly encouraged in their faith. This opened a door to compassionate communication with God. God had even more to speak into this young man's life, edifying, exhorting, and comforting him.

~~~

I'm all clean. Now what?
~~~

6. Make Your Requests Known

I previously mentioned that the primary Greek word for *prayer* is *pros-yookhomahee*. The root word *pros* means "to draw alongside." The second root element of the word for prayer is *yookhomahee*, meaning "to make your wishes known."

Consider this picture of praying to God: You approach the great doors of the throne room. The doors open, and you enter. The throne room is full of people. The king is sitting on the throne, busily conducting business. You approach, and as a servant, you reverently kneel before him. The king looks down and sees you. He smiles and motions to you, saying, "Come join me, my son/daughter." You get up and approach the king. The king sets aside all other business and gets up to meet you, saying, "Yes, child, come walk with me and let your wishes be known." God is our king, our father, and our friend.

God is the provider, and we make our requests known to Him. His desire is for us to call out to Him. But more than hearing our requests for needs and wants, He desires that we want to meet face to face. We dialogue with Him, desiring His limitless wisdom while believing He is willing and trustworthy to respond.

Certainly, there are limits as to what we mortals can understand. According to Romans 11:33, *"Oh, the depth of the riches both of the wisdom and knowledge of God! How unsearchable are His judgments and His ways past finding out!"* Yet I believe this verse is more about reinforcing the truth that there is nothing we can possibly counsel God on. Paul continues in Romans 12:2 to beseech us to renew our mind, *"that we may prove (discern) what is that good and acceptable and perfect will of God."*

Clearly, God beckons us to seek His wisdom in James 1:5-8, *"If any of you lacks wisdom, let him ask of God, who gives to all liberally and without reproach, and it will be given to him."*

And in Colossians 2:2-3 Paul expresses God's desire that we attain *"all riches of the full assurance of understanding, to the knowledge of the mystery of God, both of the Father and of Christ, in whom are hidden all the treasures of wisdom and knowledge."*

Jesus took it further, saying in John 14:13-14, *"And whatever you ask in My name, that I will do, that the Father may be glorified in the Son If you ask anything in My name, I will do it."* This is an exciting passage in which Jesus promises He will do *anything* you ask. Anything?

No, the qualifier is that we come to God to pray for things that *"the Father may be glorified in the Son,"* requesting that Jesus would share our desire to see these things fulfilled *in His name*. (Certainly, *'whatever'* includes wisdom and knowledge)

Psalm 37:4 highlights being granted the desires that are shared desires with our Lord: *"Delight yourself also in the Lord, And He shall give you the desires of your heart."* You are praying because you are both of one mind and heart, as Paul urged in Philippians 2:5, *"Let this mind be in you which was also in Christ Jesus,"*

Taking the Time to Hear His Answers

When I worked in the corporate world, we brought in experts in their fields to share their wisdom and insights. All too often, our team would fill the time touting our accomplishments and knowledge. At times, I'd want to shout, "Just shut up and listen!" I feel like that is how it is in our prayer times. We do a lot of asking and then get up to leave just when God is about to provide answers, and we walk away.

Remember, if you are praying with the desire to hear God's voice, then this is a time for listening. Let your requests be for God's wisdom and insight, and then be quiet. Leave time for silence so you can hear what He has to say. God may want to speak into what's on your mind, so be open to whatever God may want to offer. When you've concluded requesting, *stop talking and listen to Him!*

Testimonial 6
Stabbing at the Wood

As I prayed for a man in the church prayer room, the image came to my mind of someone angry and frustrated, holding a knife and repeatedly stabbing down into a rough piece of wood. The person was trying to stab something on the other side of the wood, but could not get through the piece of wood. *Oh boy! What do I do with this?*

The man admitted that he was dealing with some legal issues and other general life struggles. After praying for peace and favor, I shared the knife imagery along with Psalm 121:7-8, *"The Lord shall preserve you from all evil; He shall preserve your soul. The Lord shall preserve your going out and your coming in. From this time forth, and even forevermore."*

He stared at me and shook his head. "How did you know?" He shared that the legal trouble was because he was being accused of threatening a family member with a knife.

He explained that, in the heat of an

argument, he had picked up a knife but never actually attacked the other person with it. Even in his deep anger, something had caused him to immediately put the knife back down. But still, the family member was pressing charges.

Once again, God was exposing His perspective of reality. God saw the situation and circumstances. His intervention was the wooden cross He had died on, preventing the man from actually wielding the knife. The man prayed to give his life to Christ and that God would be his protector even from himself, *"From this time forth, and even forevermore."*

God then became this man's support, giving him favor in the legal system and helping him heal the source of his anger. God's reality worked to provide healing and restoration within his family.

~~~

Now lean into God's rhema.
~~~

7. Rhema

In the New Testament, there are two key words translated as *word*: *logos* and *rhema*. Here, we'll focus on the *rhema* of God.

Rhema is defined as an utterance. It is a matter or topic of narration. It comes from the root word *rheo*, meaning to utter, to speak, or to say. The idea is one of pouring forth—the spoken word flowing extemporaneously. *Rhema* is considered by many to be God's voice speaking directly to a person's mind, soul, and spirit. Below are examples of its use in Scripture:

- Hebrews 1:3: *"Who being the brightness of His glory and the express image of His person, and upholding all things by the word of His power, when He had by Himself purged our sins, sat down at the right hand of the Majesty on high."*
- Hebrews 6:5-6: *"For it is impossible for those who were once enlightened, and have tasted the heavenly gift, and have become partakers of the Holy Spirit,*

and have tasted the good word of God and the powers of the age to come."

- Romans 10:17: *"So then faith comes by hearing, and hearing by the word of God."*
- Ephesians 5:25-26: *"Husbands, love your wives, just as Christ also loved the church and gave Himself for her, that He might sanctify and cleanse her with the washing of water by the word."*
- Ephesians 6:17: *"And take the helmet of salvation, and the sword of the Spirit, which is the word of God."*
- 1 Peter 1:23: *"Having been born again, not of corruptible seed but incorruptible, through the word of God which lives and abides forever."*
- Acts 2:14: *(The use of rhema referring to Peter's voice.) "But Peter, standing up with the eleven, raised his voice and said to them, "Men of Judea and all who dwell in Jerusalem, let this be known to you, and heed my words."*

God Speaking in the New Testament?

Below are just a sample of New Testament examples of God's *rhema*:

- Ananias – Acts 9:10: "*Now there was a disciple in Damascus named Ananias. The Lord said to him in a vision, "Ananias," and he replied, "Here I am, Lord."*
- Paul – Acts 18:9: "*One night the Lord spoke to Paul in a vision: 'Do not be afraid; keep on speaking, do not be silent.*" And in 1 Corinthians 11:23, "*For I received from the Lord that which I also delivered to you . . .* "
- Mary – Luke 1:28-30: "*And having come in, the angel said to her, 'Rejoice, highly favored one, the Lord is with you; blessed are you among women!" But when she saw him, she was troubled at his saying, and considered what manner of greeting this was. Then the angel said to her, "Do not be afraid, Mary, for you have found favor with God."*
- Joseph – God spoke to him through dreams in Matthew 1:20: "*But while he thought about these things, behold, an angel of the Lord appeared to him in a dream.*"
- Philip with the Ethiopian – Acts

8:26 & 29, "*Now an angel of the Lord spoke to Philip, saying. . .*" and in verse 29, "*Then the Spirit said to Philip, "Go near and overtake this chariot.*"

God Has Always Spoken Directly to His People

We know that God has spoken directly to His people through *rhema* over the centuries, as documented in the Old and New Testaments and attested to by His saints. If it is indeed God's voice, then it will always be consistent with His written word, the Bible.

There are many other biblical examples of God's *rhema* spoken to His people. Some believe it stopped with the adoption of the scriptural canon, but not in my experience. Nor is it in the experience of many reliable Christians I know.

Throughout the Bible, there are exampples from both the Old and New Testament of God speaking directly to His people: Abraham, Hagar, Jacob, Enoch, Moses, Aaron, Isaiah, Nehemiah, Mary, Paul, Peter, Barnabus and most significantly, Jesus as a man. In every book of the Bible, you can find either God speaking to man or a reference to man's ability to hear from God.

We even celebrate this conversational relationship in many of our hymns. For example, "In The Garden" repeats Psalm 18:1: "He walks with me, and He talks with me."

Receiving the *Rhema*

Rhema: once you are in a posture and mindset to receive, ask God to come and speak to your mind and spirit. *Then be quiet and listen.*

- Be a ready writer. Psalm 45:1 says, *"My heart is overflowing with a good theme; I recite my composition concerning the King; My tongue is the pen of a ready writer."* Write down what comes to mind. As any images or words enter your thoughts, ask questions about what they mean and who they may be for. *Make it a dialogue.*
- Ask and keep asking as Jesus said in Matthew 7:7, *"Ask, and it will be given to you; seek, and you will find; knock, and it will be opened to you."* Test the spirits.
- One exercise is to write down the questions you ask God. After you ask the question, start writing the answer and keep writing, letting Him finish His responses. Ask more questions and let God provide answers as you continue writing.

Something Different About How Jesus Prayed

What did the disciples see that was

different about the way Jesus prayed? The difference was two-fold. First, Jesus was relational in His communication with the Heavenly Father. Second, His prayers proved powerful and effective.

We emphasize the importance of being in "relationship" with God, and we are correct to do so. Yet, if it is all about a relationship, then what would psychologists say is perhaps the most important aspect of any healthy relationship? The answer is simple: two-way communication.

Yet in prayer, we often find ourselves doing all the talking as stated earlier. Once again consider the old adage, "We were made with two ears and one mouth. We should be listening twice as much as we speak." As I read through the Bible, I believe that ratio holds true. God encourages us through His written word to listen to Him twice as often as He encourages us to speak to Him. Jesus repeatedly said, *"He who has ears to hear, let him hear!"*

Should We Rely on Hearing God's Voice?

Is it possible that reading the Bible is not the only way to hear God's voice? Possibly. Jesus seems to indicate this might be the case, saying in John 5:37-40,

> *"And the Father Himself, who sent Me, has testified of Me. You have neither heard His voice at any*

> *time, nor seen His form. But you do not have His word abiding in you, because whom He sent, Him you do not believe. You search the Scriptures, for in them you think you have eternal life; and these are they which testify of Me. But you are not willing to come to Me (hear me) that you may have life."*

Earlier in John 5:24, Jesus declared how one attains eternal life, *"... he who hears My word* (spoken by the Logos) *and believes in Him who sent Me has everlasting life"* (emphasis added). Life is not only found in the written word but also in hearing the living word—both are alive and channels to hear God's voice.

Is it Impossible to Turn Away from God?

The writer of Hebrews says that it is impossible to turn away from God after having *"...tasted the heavenly gift, and have become partakers of the Holy Spirit, and have tasted the good word (rhema) of God and the powers of the age to come"* (Hebrews 6:5-6, emphasis added).

And in Romans 10:17, it indicates that our very faith (*pistis*: faith, belief, trust, confidence; fidelity, faithfulness) originates by hearing God's spoken word (*rhema*). Ephesians 6:17 says that the sword supplied by the Spirit is God's word (*rhema*) spoken to us.

These scriptures highlight important concepts for Christ-followers. God's spoken word (*rhema*): 1) locks in our connection to God; while 2) is the source of our faith in God; and 3) is our weapon to do battle with the enemy.

How Will I Know It's God's Voice?

Jamie Winship from *Living Fearless* addressed this when he wrote, "You may ask, "Jamie, how will I know it's God speaking and not my own mind?" You will know it's God speaking because whatever it is you sense from the Holy Spirit will be encouraging, it will align with Scripture, and it won't involve accusation or condemnation. And, whatever you hear, think, or sense from the Holy Spirit should resonate with you."[13]

Testing the *Rhema*

Above all, you test what you're hearing against what you have grown to know from Scripture to be the peculiar concerning the quality, spirit or content of God's voice. Stay true to God's written word!

What should you do if you receive something that you trust is from God? Here are four tests to check it out:

1. Impressions of the Spirit: A sense that God is directing us. Acts 17:28; 2 Peter 1:21
2. Circumstances: Meyer in *The Secret of Guidance* states, "The

circumstances of our daily life are to us an infallible indication of God's will, when they concur with the inward promptings of the spirit and with the word of God."[14]

3. Independent counsel from reliable sources experienced in hearing God's voice.
4. Most importantly: The Bible, conforming to the fundamental truths of Scripture (see Psalm 111:7-8; 2 Kings 22).

Testimonial 7
I've Got This

Some of the most challenging people to pray for and to hear God's voice for are those closest to us—our family. My take on this is because they are just that—too close to us. I find it so hard to set my own thoughts and desires aside to hear God.

In particular, it is challenging with our children. They are all on their own journey, with spiritual ups and downs, as God pursues them and challenges them about His reality in their lives. Praying for them is a very real test of perseverance.

With one of our adult children, we had been growing anxious about a deepening relationship they were in. Through what I can only describe as "supernatural" means, we discovered that the other person was already not faithful and had a bad dating reputation. We had shared what we had learned with our child, but they refused to believe it, and it only seemed to draw the two closer together.

Then, as they approached an anniversary of their relationship, we grew concerned that a proposal was imminent. We prayed about intervening, and my wife and I agreed that the first thing the next morning, I would call.

The next morning, I got up early and began to pray, asking God for the words I should use when I called. I wasn't asking whether I should or shouldn't call, but just exactly what to say.

What I clearly heard back is, "I've got this." *What? Really, Lord? You'll take care of it?* I heard again, "Yes. I've got this."

My immediate joy turned to concern: *But, Lord, you know if I tell this to my wife, she'll think I'm just wimping out. She knows I'm not very good at confrontation and may think I'm using God to avoid making the call.*

Once again, I heard, "I've got this."

So, I waited for my wife to come down to the kitchen and tentatively shared what the Lord had told me. I was never so blessed at her response. She merely said, "Okay."

We prayed together that God would speak into both hearts and intervene in whatever way He thought best. Within an hour, we were shocked to see our child calling us. We answered and heard an extremely upset and emotional voice declaring that they had just broken up. Their relationship was over.

It took everything in our power to remain compassionate and caring as my wife and I restrained ourselves from openly praising God. Once again, God's voice was reassuring us that He was at work. He didn't tell us what He was doing, but challenged us to trust in His ways.

~~~

Next: Take the rhema to the logos!
~~~

8. *Logos*

Logos is defined as something said, including the thought, a topic, or subject of discourse; the divine expression (Jesus); preaching, reckoning, speech, talk, or utterance; the spoken word prepared as in a speech.

Logos, like *rhema*, often refers to the spoken word, but it comes in the form of a prepared speech or teaching, more as the expression of a person's character and intellect. It is almost universally considered to refer to the written word of God. It appears much more often than *rhema*, which may lend credence to God's emphasis on Scripture as His primary means of communication.

I believe that God speaks most often and most reliably through His written word, the Bible. God's written word, the Bible, is alive and the absolute primary source for fully knowing God and hearing from God.

One of the powerful "awakenings" I have had on my journey is that if I'm listening to God's voice and being disciplined to go to Scripture with what I'm hearing, then God's written word becomes even more meaningful and alive. Conversely, Bill Hybels from

The Power of a Whisper says, "When you increase your biblical engagement, you increase the odds that you'll hear from God."[15]

Below are just a few examples of the use of *logos* in Scripture:

- John 1:1: "*In the beginning was the Word, and the Word was with God, and the Word was God.*"
- John 1:14: "*And the Word became flesh and dwelt among us, and we beheld His glory, the glory as of the only begotten of the Father, full of grace and truth.*"
- John 5:24: "*Most assuredly, I say to you, he who hears My word and believes in Him who sent Me has everlasting life, and shall not come into judgment, but has passed from death into life.*"
- Matthew 24:35: "*Heaven and earth will pass away, but My words will by no means pass away.*"
- Hebrews 4:12: "*For the word of God is living and powerful, and sharper than any two-edged sword, piercing even to the division of soul and spirit, and of joints and marrow, and is a*

discerner of the thoughts and intents of the heart."

- Acts 4:31: *"And when they had prayed, the place where they were assembled together was shaken; and they were all filled with the Holy Spirit, and they spoke the word of God with boldness."*
- 2 Timothy 2:15: *"Be diligent to present yourself approved to God, a worker who does not need to be ashamed, rightly dividing the word of truth."*
- Acts 2:22: The use of *logos* refers to Peter's voice – *"Men of Israel, hear these words: Jesus of Nazareth, a Man attested by God to you by miracles, wonders, and signs which God did through Him in your midst, as you yourselves also know. . ."*

Logos versus *Rhema*

As I go through Scripture to identify a pattern for the use of each, it seems that one (rhema) is identifying a dialogue. In contrast, the other identifies a logically constructed order of words: a logical message. *Logos* can be most accurately translated as logic.

Still, both words refer to the spoken word. What this suggests to me is that, given the two words with different meanings, God's word (or voice) can come in various forms—all-powerful, effective, and important for fully engaging with God. To me, it opens the door for God to speak through means other than the Bible, but always in a way consistent with the Bible. We can trust in both sources because we have come to know His voice.

Dallas Willard states in his book, *Hearing God*, "But there is nothing in scripture to indicate that the biblical modes of God's communication with humans have been superseded or abolished by either the presence of the church or the close of the scriptural canon. This is simply a fact, just as it is simply a fact that God's children have continued up to the present age to find themselves addressed by God in most of the ways he commonly addressed biblical characters."[16]

Let me state it one more time:
The holy Bible is the bedrock and foundation for God's revelation of who He is and for our relationship with God.

We can spend a lifetime in the Bible and continually discover new aspects of God's truth within it. It is an amazing piece of spiritual communication technology! God's written word, The Bible, is alive and the absolute primary source for fully knowing God and hearing from Him.

Pulled into the Power of *Logos*

Thank God that He speaks directly to

our spirit. But I find hearing God is at its best when we ask God to speak further through His written word.

After praying and listening, open your Bible to your current reading location. (Do not play Scripture roulette; proactively choose a place.) Continue reading and see if God brings further clarity to what you heard right there at that moment. If words/images jump out, grab your concordance and do a relevant word study. And don't forget to take notes.

If the message is for another person, when you share it, encourage the recipient to meditate on it as the beginning of their own dialogue with God, using it as a conversation starter. Whenever possible, ask God to lead you to Scripture that ties the *rhema* back to *logos*—tying the message to Scripture.

Jamie Winship in *Living Fearless* writes, "Don't only read the Bible in some formulaic pattern. Instead, ask God, "What does this say to me? How is this related to my identity? What do you want me to know?"[17]

In John 10:14 and 27, Jesus said His people know His voice. Do we recognize his voice as familiar, like James Earl Jones or Morgan Freeman? Or do we know it by *the uniquely peculiar quality, spirit, and content* of what God would say?

Rarely have I actually heard a voice. To me, God's voice comes in the form of thoughts and images. Then I test these thoughts and images against what I have grown to *know* to be the peculiar quality, spirit, and content of God's character—the character of Jesus found in the Gospels and described throughout Scripture. Some key Scriptures are:

- 1 Corinthians 14:3: "*But he who prophesies speaks edification and exhortation and comfort to men.*" Under the terms of the New Covenant, God's voice is about building us up, encouraging us to move out and assuring us that He is with us.
- Galatians 5:22-23: "*But the fruit of the Spirit is love, joy, peace, longsuffering, kindness, goodness, faithfulness, gentleness, self-control. Against such there is no law.*"

The simple test for any New Covenant message that God has for another person or for me is that it must edify, exhort, and comfort as well as be an expression of the full fruit of the Spirit—and a reflection of the character of Jesus. If it fails the test, ask God for further clarification, or put it on the shelf, or simply throw it out.

Testimonial 8
Looking to 'Sign'

I began attending a Christian men's morning meeting where I sat at a table with a group of guys I didn't know. At a time of prayer, I asked God, *Is there anything You want me to speak to someone here?*

I saw in my mind's eye an image of a man sitting at a desk with a piece of paper in front of him that required his signature. To me, it seemed akin to considering whether to sign a legal document, such as a loan agreement. He was hesitant to sign it, repeatedly pushing it away, and then drawing it back. I heard the words "sign it."

Okay, Lord, *Who's this for?* I looked around the table and got the impression it was for a certain man across from me. When the meeting ended, I went up to him and asked if I could share something that I thought the Lord had for him. He tentatively said, "Yeah, sure."

I shared the imagery with him and said I didn't know exactly what it meant, but if he was facing a "go/no-go" decision, I think God wanted him to go for it. Sign it! I was then led to share Isaiah 7:11, *"Ask a sign for yourself from the Lord your God; ask it either in the depth or in the height above."*

I then prayed that God would continue to speak to him, and it would prove to be a blessing. I concluded, and he seemed a bit stunned, but he thanked me. Maybe it landed, maybe not? I was faithful, and I left.

A few weeks later, I scheduled breakfast with another man from that men's group, for whom God had given me something impactful to share. We met at the local diner, and he said he had just called a friend of his to join us. Fine.

In walked the guy I had told God said to "sign it!" He came right up to me and shook my hand, saying, "If my friend had mentioned any name other than Dave, I wouldn't have come." He had remembered my name from my name tag, and when his friend mentioned Dave, he thought it might be me. He then shared the impact of God's *rhema*.

He was a Christian but admitted that he drank a bit too much. He didn't really see it as a problem. But the night before the men's meeting, he had a night playing pickleball and hard drinking with his buddies. That morning, he decided he would 'take a pause' from drinking for 40 days. He included in that 'pause' smoking cigars and a permanent stop to chewing tobacco.

An hour before the men's meeting, he drew up a paper listing 40 days' worth of blocks, each with a line for him to sign off on every day he did not drink, smoke, or chew, planning to pause for 40 days. Then, a few hours later, if he was equivocating, the Lord stepped in and told him to "sign it."

At the diner, he slid a paper across the table to me with about three weeks' worth of signatures, signed every day since God had spoken to him. Wow!

God further encouraged him as I shared Job 31:35 (NLT), *"If only someone would listen to me! Look, I will sign my name to my defense. Let the Almighty answer me. Let my accuser write out the charges against me."*

As a side note, the document I had seen in my mind appeared to be a loan instrument. The man's profession? Financial lending. Cool!

~~~

I received God's rhema and logos. What's next?
~~~

9. Doers of The Word

James 1:21-22 and 26 state,
"Therefore lay aside all filthiness and overflow of wickedness, and receive with meekness the implanted word (logou), which is able to save your souls. But be doers of the word (logou), and not hearers only, deceiving yourselves. . . . For as the body without the spirit is dead, so faith without works is dead also" (emphasis added).

Whether you sense a message is for you or for someone else, act on it or share it with those willing to hear it. The Hebrew verb sh'ma (שְׁמַע) is often translated as *hear.* It means much more than just hearing or listening, but rather to "hear and respond appropriately"—to hear and then to act. The Greek word for *obedience* means *attentive hearkening.*

Author Bill Hybels encourages acting on what you *hear,* "If you lower the ambient noise of your life and listen expectantly for those whispers of God, your ears will hear them. And when you follow their lead, your world will be rocked."[18]

Jesus warns of the foolishness to hear and not to put it into action in Matthew 7:26, (NIV) *"But everyone who hears these words (logos) of mine and does not put them into practice is like a foolish man who built his house on sand."* (The ramifications only get worse.)

In 1 Samuel 15:22, God says, *"So Samuel said: 'Has the Lord as great delight in burnt offerings and sacrifices, As in obeying the voice of the Lord? Behold, to obey is better than sacrifice, And to heed than the fat of rams.'"* When we hear God's voice and act on it, we are stepping out in faith, and God is pleased.

Hebrews 11:6 states, *"But without faith it is impossible to please Him, for he who comes to God must believe that He is, and that He is a rewarder of those who diligently seek Him."* The Greek word for *diligently seek* is *ekzētousin*, which means to seek out, but also to *require of* or *to need for a particular purpose.*

If the rhema is a word for:

- You: If the word is for you, it may be a word of comfort or insight into the world around you. Let it bless you and bring you joy. But if it requires action on your part, strive to follow through. It is for your benefit or for those around you, but it also affects your ability to hear. If God speaks and you ignore it, I'm not sure you can expect to be rewarded with hearing more from God.

- Others: When you receive something for others, you don't have to fully understand it. Always pray that God would use it to speak into their lives. God will reward your faithfulness, even if it doesn't seem to have a significant impact on those you share it with.

Note: What I hear from God is often clearer as a message for others, but some element of that message often boomerangs right back at me.

Testimonial 9
Pulled to Safe Harbor

The other man I mentioned in my previous testimonial was another experience of God's *rhema*. When I started attending the same Christian men's meeting, I began sitting with a young man over 90 years old. He is Greek, and my wife is Greek, so we had that in common.

At one point, we had a discussion at our table, and it became clear to me that this man had never taken the step to give his life to Christ. I prayed, and God gave me an image of a man in an open rowboat, vigorously rowing but being tossed about in a storm. The only thing keeping the boat from overturning was a taut rope tied to the bow, which was drawing the boat forward. Though the man couldn't see it, Jesus was on the shore, pulling the boat to safety.

Isaiah 41:10 came to mind: *"Fear not, for I am with you; Be not dismayed, for I am your God. I will strengthen you, Yes, I will help you, I will uphold you with My righteous right hand."*

I shared this with him, and I could see his mind churning. He said, "That happened to me." He detailed that as a young man in Greece, he was on his first fishing boat and hoped to one day become a licensed captain. In the evening, the other sailors on the boat handed him the wheel, told him to keep a certain course, and they all went to sleep. A sudden storm hit, and he had no idea what to do. The boat was being battered and tossed. He thought for sure they would crash on the rocky shore.

When the sailors woke up, they were shocked to find the boat safely in their harbor. They incredulously asked the young man, "How did you get here? This is impossible." He shrugged. He didn't know how it happened.

This man now knew that it was God who had miraculously brought him to the safe harbor. He had been coming to this Christian men's group for several years, enjoying the speakers and the fellowship, but doubting the reality of the God the other men shared. Now, God's *rhema* convinced him of God's reality through Jesus, and he prayed to give his life to Christ.

~~~

I tried, but it seemed awkward and foolish. What do I do?
~~~

10. Perseverance

Hebrews 10:36 – "*You need to persevere so that when you have done the will of God, you will receive what he has promised.*"

Not everything we hear and share will land. It takes perseverance to get our flesh out of the way so we can hear God more clearly. But the more we faithfully practice this, the more it becomes a practice in which God rewards our faithfulness.

Jamie Winship puts it this way: "Being able to hear God is a new skill. It's like learning how to understand Morse code. You have to practice; it's a discipline. Or it's like tuning in to a radio frequency. You turn the knob, but there are so many voices and so much static and noise. Then, finally, you find the station with the voice you recognize. The frequency resonates with your heart, and you keep fine-tuning it until the voice is crystal clear. You learn to hear God's voice above all other voices."[19]

Comer in *Practicing the Way* also encourages persevering, "Stay with it. The one non-negotiable rule of prayer is this: Keep showing up."[20]

Prophesy for All to Their Measure of Faith

In 1 Corinthians 14:5, it's written, "*I wish you all spoke with tongues, but even more that you prophesied.*" This tells me that God speaking to us so that he may speak through us to others is available to all His people.

But Scripture qualifies this availability to different degrees in Romans 12, verses 3b and 6 saying, "*... God has dealt to each one a measure of faith. . . Having then gifts differing according to the grace that is given to us, let us use them: if prophecy, let us prophesy in proportion to our faith.*"

It is a mysterious mix of our desire and diligence, along with the measure of grace and faith that God distributes to each one of us. If you have the desire and exert the diligence required, then God will grant greater levels of faith and grace—always looking unto Jesus, the author and finisher of our faith (Hebrews 12:2). The more you practice, the more you will be in-the-practice of hearing God.

Practicing to Be In-The-Practice

Ephesians 4:12-13 states,

> *For the perfecting of the saints, for the work of the ministry, for the edifying of the body of Christ: Till we all come in the unity of the faith,*

> *and of the knowledge of the Son of God, unto a perfect man, unto the measure of the stature of the fullness of Christ.*

What about the concept of practicing our faith? In Christian circles, when discussing spiritual matters, we often use the phrase "practicing our faith." I've often wondered about the meaning of the term. In Christian vernacular, people are talking about "being active in their life with Christ" or "applying what they believe." But the word *practice* has a bit of a double meaning in English.

Definitions of Practice

Here are the two definitions for practice, and notice the nuance:

1. The word's earliest meaning was 'to pursue or be engaged in a particular occupation, profession, skill, or art' as in the practice of law or medicine.
2. Sometime later, it was recorded as meaning *to perform an activity or exercise a skill repeatedly or regularly in order to acquire, improve or maintain proficiency*. This is the meaning it most commonly has today.

So, when we exercise (practice) our faith, are we merely *practicing* or *in-the-practice*?

I certainly know that exercising faith is inevitably about trusting God as we step into the unknown. To excel in anything, we need basic elements such as studying, observing, exercising, testing, and performing.

Consider something like a medical *practice*. A medical student spends years studying, learning, and testing to develop their knowledge and skill, practicing their craft to then become fully licensed in the "practice" of medicine.

But what does that mean as a Christ-follower? If I say that I am in-the-practice, it suggests that I am fully matured and an expert in the things of faith—the exercise of spiritual disciplines and of spiritual gifts. Unfortunately, I don't feel like I'm in a position to put up a shingle to declare I'm fully "in-the-practice."

But what about the idea that we practice to develop certain skills? Does that not relate to the things of God in the spiritual realm—developing proficiency in spiritual disciplines and gifts? What about the concept of testing our faith? Testing is a critical component of fully exercising and practicing our faith.

Comer writes, "Jesus also assumes that living his Way is going to take practice. . . Jesus begins and ends the Sermon on the Mount with a call to practice."[21]

In Matthew 7:24 (NIV) Jesus emphasized our need to practice to be in the practice, declaring, *"Therefore everyone who hears these words of mine and puts them into practice is like a wise man who built his house on the rock."*

Who's Testing Who?

God is not testing us to understand where our faith is. He is pulling back to allow us to test ourselves. We see a great biblical example of this in 2 Chronicles 32, where it notes that *"God left him (Hezekiah) to try him, that he might know all that was in his heart."*

At times, God stands back to let us test the extent of our true faith in Him. In Greek, the word for *testing* is *dokimion*—that by which something is tried or proved. We try/test it to prove it to ourselves.

Where Can We Go to Test Spiritual Matters?

This is what I see as a function of the body of Christ: to lovingly exhort one another to greater levels of faith, experience, and knowledge of the living God. First Thessalonians 2:11 reports, *"As you know how we exhorted, and comforted, and charged every one of you, as a father does his own children,"*

There are typically many great examples of this in most church communities—exhorting the study of God's written Word, applying God's word by serving one another and the community, sending, giving, and praying. All this is to more fully know a greater reality of God in our lives and then to have God impact the world through us more powerfully.

Paul writes about the church's role of exhortation in Colossians 1:9-11, *"For this reason we also, since the day we heard it, do not cease to pray for you, and to ask that you may be filled with the knowledge of His will in all wisdom and spiritual understanding; that you may walk worthy of the Lord, fully pleasing Him, being fruitful in every good work and increasing in the knowledge of God; strengthened with all might, according to His glorious power, for all patience and longsuffering with joy."*

The Greek word for *knowledge* is *epignosis*: the precise and correct understanding and the knowledge of things ethical and divine. Paul's writings encourage us to grow in our faith, trust, and wisdom, but as previously highlighted, most importantly, in our *knowledge* of God.

Often, we limit that to intellectual knowledge, but I believe it may be more about knowing Him relationally. We then grow in our faith and trust, and in our wisdom, in the person we have come to know. Good examples of this are found in:

- Ephesians 1:17: *"That the God of our Lord Jesus Christ, the Father of glory, may give unto you the spirit of wisdom and revelation in the knowledge of him."*

- Ephesians 4:13: *"Till we all come in the unity of the faith, and of the knowledge of the Son of God, unto a perfect man, unto the measure of the stature of the fullness of Christ."*

How can we achieve the "fullness of Christ" if we don't confidently know Him?

Spiritual Laboratories

So, consider whether we give adequate room for testing and exploring the spiritual gifts God has for each of us as we seek to fully know God in our community of Christ-followers?

Jamie Winship in *Living Fearless* writes, "Remember that as the people in Acts start living their lives under the direction of the Spirit of God, it's an experiment. They have never experienced anything like this before."[22]

Do we create spiritual laboratories where we make space, leaving greater room for the movement of the Holy Spirit? In these spaces, while standing on the bedrock of God's written Word, with the guidance of our spiritual overseers, we exhort one another to test/stretch the practice of our faith by engaging with God to expect something beyond the limits we have set—to expect more. Jamie Winship also writes, "This is the definition of true accountability, affirming and nudging people forward in their true identity and destiny."[23]

The more we test the limits of our faith and practice, stretching it, the more God shows up to reward our diligent seeking of Him. We experience the reality of this dynamic to test what we practice so that we become more fully In-the-Practice.

Developing your spiritual listening skills is not necessarily easy and requires discipline:

- 1 Thessalonians 5:19-21: *"Do not quench the Spirit. Do not despise prophecies. Test all things; hold fast what is good."*
- 1 John 4:1: *"Beloved, do not believe every spirit, but test the spirits, whether they are of God; because many false prophets have gone out into the world."*
- 2 Timothy 2:15: *"Be diligent to present yourself approved to God, a worker who does not need to be ashamed, rightly dividing the word of truth."*

Testimonial 10
Letting Arrows In

I was at a Sunday service and as the pastor was teaching, the word 'bulletproof' came to my mind. I believed it was meant for the pastor, so after the service I shared with him that the Lord wanted him to know he was bulletproof. He smiled, nodded, and simply said, "Okay."

I knew that this pastor had been under a lot of pressure during the pandemic and the rise of the Black Lives Matter movement, as he resisted those pressures. Romans 12:2 came to mind, *"And do not be conformed to this world, but be transformed by the renewing of your mind, that you may prove what is that good and acceptable and perfect will of God."*

Yet something "stuck in my craw" and I continued to pray and meditate on the meaning of being bulletproof. I got the impression that its meaning had to do with God giving the pastor the strength to hold up the large, heavy shield of faith to repel the slings and arrows of the enemy.

At the same time, there was a potential downside to being bulletproof. God wanted him to discern which arrows came from God's bow, to penetrate the pastor's heart. I wondered if there was a hardness that God wanted to penetrate?

There are arrows intended to pierce our hearts with God's love, affection, and guidance. The shield, which is intended to protect us from the enemy, should not repel what God intends for our good and for His glory. I relayed this to the pastor and told him to "Rejoice! God's got you where He wants you and there's a target on your heart!"

I shared Ephesians 6:16, *"Above all, taking the shield of faith with which you will be able to quench all the fiery darts of the wicked one,"* and Isaiah 26:3, *"You will keep him in perfect peace, Whose mind is stayed on You, Because he trusts in You."*

Shortly thereafter, the pastor was caught up in a public confrontation with a powerful social media commentator. Clearly, the enemy was slinging arrows at him, and it was a difficult time. But the pastor took what I had shared to heart and was willing to let God's arrows penetrate his heart to soften it and to see where he may have erred in this exchange. This word and what God spoke through others into the pastor's life during this painful episode sustained and even refreshed and renewed him.

The pastor further testified that, "The

word, *bulletproof* was a strong source of encouragement to me because it meant my Heavenly Father loves me so much that He was giving me a warning. Even though I didn't initially understand it, I would in time. That's what's amazing about receiving a prophetic word. Sometimes we want the interpretation right then and there, but I got the interpretation afterwards, which was better than getting it immediately. It's a great reminder today of progressive prophetic interpretation. We are used to microwave results, but sometimes we need to wait on the Lord."

~~~

In Matthew 13:16, Jesus teaches His disciples about blessings we uniquely have in Christ: *"But blessed are your eyes for they see, and your ears for they hear."*
~~~

Final Notes

The ten-step process to develop your ability to hear God shouldn't be cumbersome. Perhaps you may linger in some areas, but 'hearing God' prayer requires swiftly flowing through the steps to spend more time listening and then in the meditation/study of God's written Word.

It is not much different from the classic A.C.T.S. prayer model of adoration, confession, thanksgiving, and supplication, but adds the letter L for listening. Much of this is reflected in Philippians 4:6-7:

> *Be anxious for nothing, but in everything by prayer and supplication, with thanksgiving, let your requests be made known to God; and the peace of God, which surpasses all understanding, will guard your hearts and minds through Christ Jesus.*
>
> With the hearing comes the peace.
>
> Reminders:
>
> - God is not a cosmic butler. God is gracious to speak to us, but is

under no obligation. At times, His silence can be as impactful as any spoken word.

- Don't force a word. We are not hearing God for others' entertainment or to demonstrate our spirituality or giftedness. (In Matthew 16, Jesus refused to perform miracles as a "show," spectacle, or on-demand proof.)
- Test all things. First Thessalonians 5:19-22 states, *"Do not quench the Spirit. Do not despise prophecies. Test all things; hold fast what is good. Abstain from every form of evil."*
- We are not built to be robots. God's will is that we ourselves, with Christ living inside us, should have a great part in determining our path through this life.
- Jeremiah 17:10: *"I the LORD, search the heart, I test the mind, Even to give every man according to his ways, According to the fruit of his doings."*
- Galatians 2:20: *"I have been crucified with Christ; it is no longer I who live, but Christ lives in me; and the life which I now live in the flesh I live by*

> *faith in the Son of God, who loved me and gave Himself for me."*

Infallibility Not Required Under the New Covenant

As I mentioned before, I believe New Covenant prophesy is less about specific step-by-step instruction from God or about foretelling the future but more about engaging with God in a relationship while building up the body of Christ. First Corinthians 14:3 says, *"But he who prophesies speaks edification and exhortation and comfort to men."*

We are not expected to be infallible. If we share something we sincerely believe we've heard from God and it proves to be wrong, we aren't subject to being stoned. Dallas Willard comments, "Infallibility, and especially infallibility in discerning the mind of God, simply does not fit the human condition. It should not be desired, much less expected, from our relationship with God."[24]

Finally, as you pursue and act on hearing God's voice, know that it is rational, enabled by God's power and love, and that we will be rewarded for courageously stepping out in faith.

- 2 Timothy 1:7: *"For God has not given us a spirit of fear, but of power and of love and of a sound mind."*
- Hebrews 11:6: *"But without*

faith it is impossible to please Him, for he who comes to God must believe that He is, and that He is a rewarder of those who diligently seek Him."

- Deuteronomy 31:6: "*Be strong and of good courage, do not fear nor be afraid of them; for the Lord your God, He is the One who goes with you. He will not leave you nor forsake you."*

Conclusion

Do you believe that God *can* speak to you? Do you believe that God *wants* to speak to you? I believe that God is speaking to us, and we are either unwilling or unable to hear. In my experience, it takes desire and the investment in time and effort to develop our spiritual listening skills as it does to grow in any healthy relationship.

Pastor Jamie Winship asked this question to a group of school administrators he spoke with, who likely doubted that God can speak to them: "How many of you can hear a voice in your head saying, *You're not good enough, you're not smart enough? That you're not talented enough or good enough at what you do?* How many of you can hear that voice?" All raised their hands.

He responded, "Good. We all agree that we can hear voices! Now, how many of you can hear a voice that says, *You are loved with an everlasting love, and you are good enough all the time?* How many can hear that voice?" None raised their hand.

Why? Is it because that voice isn't talking? No, it's because we are trained to hear that other voice.

Let's start believing that God's loving goodness is speaking. Get alone with God, loosen up, and lean into His still small voice. The more you do, the more God's still small voice can be heard through the loud turbulence and competing noise of this world.

Some Resources on the Subject of Hearing God:

- *Hearing God, Spirit of the Disciplines, Knowing Christ Today, The Divine Conspiracy* – Dallas Willard
- *Desire & Walking with God* – John Eldridge
- *The Life You Always Wanted* – John Ortberg
- *Desiring God* – John Piper
- *Experiencing God* – Henry Blackaby
- *Hearts Cry* – Jennifer Kennedy Dean
- *How to Listen to God* – Charles Stanley
- *Beloved* – Francis Chan
- *Practicing the Way: Be with Jesus. Become Like Him. Do as He Did* – John Mark Comer
- *The Power of a Whisper* – Bill Hybels: "Hearing the quiet whisper of the transcendent God is one of the most extraordinary privileges in all of life—and potentially the most transforming dynamic in the Christian faith."[25]

Notes

[1]Dallas Willard: *Knowing Christ Today. Why We Can Trust Spiritual Knowledge*, (New York, NY: HarperCollins Publishers, 2014), page 21.

[2]John Mulinde & Mark Daniel: *Prayer Altars: A Strategy That Is Changing Nations,* (Orlando, FL: Reviving Nations Publishing), page 71.

[3]Francis Chan: *Beloved*, (Colorado Springs, CO: David C. Cook, 2025), page 94.

[4]Dallas Willard: *The Allure of Gentleness*, *Defending the Faith in the Manner of Jesus,* (New York, NY: HarperCollins Publishers, 2016), page 6.

[5]Jamie Winship: *Living Fearless: Exchanging the Lies of the World for the Liberating Truth of God,* (Grand Rapids, Michigan: Revell a division of Baker Publishing Group, 2022), page 21.

[6]*Ibid*., page 69.

[7]John Mulinde & Mark Daniel: *Prayer Altars: A Strategy That Is Changing Nations,* (Orlando, FL: Reviving Nations Publishing), page 95.

[8]*Ibid*., page 93.

[9]Jamie Winship: *Living Fearless: Exchanging the Lies of the World for the Liberating Truth of God,* (Grand Rapids, Michigan: Revell a division of Baker Publishing Group, 2022), page 63.

[10]John Mark Comer: *Practicing the Way: Be with Jesus. Become Like Him. Do as He Did* (Colorado Springs, CO: WaterBrook, 2024), page 221.

[11]Dallas Willard: *The Spirit of The Disciplines, Understanding How God Changes Lives,* (New York, NY: HarperCollins Publishers, 1990), page 157.

[12]Francis Chan: *Beloved*, (Colorado Springs, CO: David C. Cook, 2025), page 104.

[13]Jamie Winship: *Living Fearless: Exchanging the Lies of the World for the Liberating Truth of God,* (Grand Rapids, Michigan: Revell a division of Baker Publishing Group, 2022), page 125.

[14]F.B. Meyer: *The Secret of Guidance,* (Chicago, IL: Moody Press), page 33.

[15]Bill Hybels: *The Power of a Whisper: Hearing God, Having the Guts to Respond*, (Grand Rapids, MI: Zondervan, 2012), page 115.

[16]Dallas Willard: *Hearing God: Developing a Conversational Relationship with God,* (Downers Grove, IL: Intervarsity Press, 1999), page 136.

[17]Jamie Winship: *Living Fearless: Exchanging the Lies of the World for the Liberating Truth of God,* (Grand Rapids, Michigan: Revell a division of Baker Publishing Group, 2022), page 79.

[18]Bill Hybels: *The Power of a Whisper: Hearing God, Having the Guts to Respond*, (Grand Rapids, MI: Zondervan, 2012), page 11.

[19]Jamie Winship: *Living Fearless: Exchanging the Lies of the World for the Liberating Truth of God,* (Grand Rapids, Michigan: Revell a division of Baker Publishing Group, 2022), page 127.

[20]John Mark Comer: *Practicing the Way: Be with Jesus. Become like him. Do as he did*, (Colorado Springs, CO: WaterBrook, 2024), page 72.

[21]*Ibid.*, page 123.

[22]Jamie Winship: *Living Fearless: Exchanging the Lies of the World for the Liberating Truth of God,* (Grand Rapids, Michigan: Revell a division of Baker Publishing Group, 2022), page 155.

[23]*Ibid.*, page 162.

[24]Dallas Willard: *Hearing God: Developing a Conversational Relationship with God,* (Downers Grove, IL: Intervarsity Press, 1999), page 240.

[25]Bill Hybels: *The Power of a Whisper: Hearing God, Having the Guts to Respond*, (Grand Rapids, MI: Zondervan, 2012), page 41.

Other Published Works by David Lee Tucker

Stone Wall Freedom Trilogy:
Part I – The Pirate
Part II – The Islander
Part III – The Slave

The Block Island Settlement Series:
The Battle of Mohegan Bluffs – Book I
The Fate of Captain John Oldham – Book II
Puritan Retribution & Manisses Destiny – Book III
Block Island Beckons – Book IV
Block Island Brotherhoods – Book V
Block Island Way of Escape - Book VI

Additional Writings

Christian Non-Fiction:

The Wigglesworth Dilemma

Christian Blog

tuckedin-lampsburning.com

Contact David Lee Tucker at

Dleetucker@gmail.com

www.ingramcontent.com/pod-product-compliance
Lightning Source LLC
LaVergne TN
LVHW010626100826
845148LV00014B/3129

* 9 7 8 1 6 3 3 6 0 3 5 8 5 *